IMAGES
of America

CALIFORNIA CAVALRY

On the Cover: In this 1941 image, the 11th Cavalry salutes the colors while in Campo. (Courtesy of Valerie Read.)

IMAGES
of America

CALIFORNIA CAVALRY

Jennifer A. Garey

ARCADIA
PUBLISHING

ISBN 978-1-4671-3110-0

Published by Arcadia Publishing
Charleston, South Carolina

Printed in the United States of America

Library of Congress Control Number: 2013944357

For all general information, please contact Arcadia Publishing:
Telephone 843-853-2070
Fax 843-853-0044
E-mail sales@arcadiapublishing.com
For customer service and orders:
Toll-Free 1-888-313-2665

Visit us on the Internet at www.arcadiapublishing.com

*To Valerie, who made it possible, and to my family,
Marty, Penny, and Phoebe.*

Contents

Acknowledgments

Thank you, Valerie Read, for the photographs of your father, a veterinarian for the 11th Cavalry, and for allowing me to share your father's memory. Penelope Luksic, for giving the text a thorough once-over; you are the best writer I know. Thank you for your patience and your tactful candor. Thank you also to Marty and Phoebe, who made my exploration into the subject possible by taking care of daily life while I stepped out of it. A thank-you goes to the staff on the fifth floor of the National Archives, College Park; each of you made this project fun. Thank you, Jared Nelson, for believing in me and putting up with me, and I also thank Arcadia Publishing for letting me do this project, even if it is a little out of scope. All images appear courtesy of the National Archives and Records Administration (NARA), with the exception of chapter four, in which all images are courtesy of Valerie Read.

I hope that I was able to share this part of American history in a way that is respectful to cavalry regiments and respectful to the Indian nations that live in California and surrounding areas. We can only hope that we do not forget or ignore history since it is one of the best ways we can learn to become better at being human.

INTRODUCTION

Mounted cavalry was a military asset in America for hundreds of years beginning in 1777 during the Revolutionary War. The first official horse-mounted cavalry, the Corps of Continental Dragoons, was initially used for reconnaissance but was later outfitted with weapons and employed as an infantry throughout the Civil War, as mounted cavalry became strategically important for both the Union and Confederate armies. Mounted cavalries were critical in war campaigns in Cuba and the Philippines and were used exclusively in the US war against Mexico and Mexican revolutionary leaders such as José Doroteo Arango Arámbula, also known as Francisco "Pancho" Villa. The mounted cavalry was also an integral part of westward expansion and the attempted removal and extermination of the nations of people indigenous to the continent.

The image of the US cavalry has become synonymous with extreme events in American military history. Under the direction of Pres. Andrew Jackson, the mounted cavalry was part of one of the worst periods in American history, the attempted genocide of America's indigenous nations.

Aside from these military acts, the mounted cavalry served noncombative roles. Cavalries assisted with the surveying of land designated as national parks and were often tasked with maintaining the security of parks. Today, the National Park Service rangers continue to emulate the dress and military structure of the mounted cavalry.

California was the site of a number of mounted cavalry camps. The unique and varied landscape of flat desert, hillside chaparral, rocky mountain passes, beaches, and sandy dunes offered a training ground like no other. A number of cavalry units originated in these diverse landscapes. A short-lived Native American Cavalry, originating in Los Angeles in 1862, was commanded by Californio rancher Don Andreas Pico. The term "native" in Native American Cavalry refers to the Californios, or Mexican-Californian people. It was speculated that these Californio *vaqueros*, known to be expert horse riders, would make formidable cavalry soldiers. The Native American Cavalry was comprised of Californio vaqueros along with Mexicans, Chileans, Sonoran, and Yaqui Indians, Germans, and Americans. It operated under various commanders, and the occasional suspicion of disloyalty, until it was disbanded in 1866. California was also home to one of the first African American cavalries. These cavalry units were known as Buffalo Soldiers, a name given by Indians as a sign of respect.

Before mechanization, the mounted cavalry was considered the fastest mobile unit, excelling in reconnaissance, scouting, and reporting. Later, used on the front lines of combat operations, the mounted cavalry was the most prestigious military outfit. During training, a soldier developed his weaponry skills and his understanding of guns, riding, and horse and mule care. Today, horses and mules are no longer used in vast numbers for military combat situations; these animals are more likely to be used by police forces, as they remain one of the best means of crowd control. The cavalry is now mechanized and unmounted, signifying 20th-century changes in military technology.

The history of the American cavalry has been romanticized in popular culture and, therefore, divorced from most of its ruthless acts. According to Paul Chaat Smith in *Everything You Know about*

Indians is Wrong, "Europeans invaded, conquered and pillaged heavily populated, developed real estate." Vine Delora, in his book *Custer Died for Your Sins*, describes the 19th-century opinion that, "because the Indian occupied large areas of land, he was considered a wild animal." The policies of the 19th-century United States were based on these prejudices and the belief in Manifest Destiny, the idea that white Americans had the right to make the world in their cultural likeness.

Though perspectives differ, when history is not recounted openly, or worse, ignored, the effects can be devastating to all. There will always be more than one perspective of any event; it is understanding the interactions of perspectives that show the whole picture.

Outlining the history of the California cavalry, battalions, and regiments between 1840 and 1941 and showing images of a time lost to advancement in military technology, *California Cavalry* has attempted to approach the topic of the cavalry from the perspective of native nations and cavalry troopers. Because California was not a state during the first half of American mounted cavalry history, the geographic regions are expanded to give context and continuity. To maintain historic accuracy, photograph locations are referred to according to the period in which the photograph was taken; for example, the text will note San Antonio, Mexico, as opposed to San Antonio, Texas, when applicable.

The subject matter of the mounted and mechanized cavalries is vast and interesting. Perhaps this small view will provide inspiration to find out more.

One

Cavalry Sent West

The photographs in this section depict the early period of California history. It was a period of power struggles between the Californio rancheros, indigenous nations, and Mexico. In 1846, Pres. James K. Polk and Secretary of War William Marcy ordered Col. Stephen W. Kearney, commander of the 1st Dragoons, the early 1st Cavalry, to march into California and seize Monterey and San Francisco. Polk and his administration wanted to ensure that, if peace agreements were made with Mexico, the United States would achieve military control of California.

Cavalry regiments sent into the Western United States were tasked with forcibly acquiring real estate, maintaining a power position through either violent means or forced treaties, and controlling newly acquired land. This included processes of attempted extermination and relocation of Native Americans, the owners of the real estate. It also included establishing military posts, towns, and rail lines to claim the land and protect the new white westward immigration across the continent, and it included the planned systematic extermination of the Plains Indians' main resource, the buffalo.

Pictured are the officers of Troops D and L of the 1st Cavalry, also known as the Machine Gun Platoon and Field Artillery Battery. From left to right are (sitting) Lieutenant Haiz; Captain Poillon, 1st Cavalry, Troop D, commander; Captain Harbord, 1st Cavalry, Troop L; Captain Hilton; and Lieutenant Van Kirk, MD; (standing) Lieutenant Kabbi, 1st Cavalry, Troop L; Lieutenant Bell, 1st Cavalry, M.C. Platoon; Lieutenant Brown, 1st Cavalry, Troop D; Lieutenant Wainwright, 1st Cavalry, Troop L; and Lieutenant Spencer, 1st Cavalry, Troop D. Hilton's dog, Tony, is also pictured. (NARA 106817.)

The 4th Cavalry Orchestra is pictured at Fort Bowie after Geronimo's surrender in 1886. Geronimo (Mescalero Chiricahua) Goyathlay was a leader of the Bedonkohe Apache Nation. In 1858, Mexican soldiers attacked and killed his mother, wife, and three children, after which he pursued and fought Mexico and the United States for several decades. Some of the people identified in the photograph are William A. Raymond, Charles Kimball, Peter Siteloronor, Thomas O'Brien, and John J. Kelley. (NARA 87373.)

Captain Keogh's horse Comanche was the sole survivor of the Custer massacre. Comanche was captured somewhere on the southern plains and brought to a remount station in St. Louis, Missouri, in 1868. There, he was broken in and then shipped to Fort Leavenworth. At the fort, he was selected to be loaded on a train bound for Ellis Station, where the 7th Cavalry was encamped. He arrived at the encampment on May 19, 1868, and caught the eye of Captain Keogh, and they were inseparable until the Battle of Little Bighorn in June 1876. (NARA 111-SC-83342.)

Originally ruled by Mexico, the Presidio in San Francisco came under the control of the United States in 1846. With the discovery of gold in California in 1849, the US government established the Presidio as a permanent military post. During the 1870s through the 1880s, the Presidio was camp to many cavalry regiments ordered to fight the Modoc Nation in Northern California and the Apache Nation in the southwest plains. (NARA 87839.)

In 1914, Gen. John J. "Black Jack" Pershing commanded the 8th Cavalry, dispatched from the Presidio to pursue Mexican revolutionary Francisco "Pancho" Villa. While Pershing was on the expedition, his wife, Frances, and their three daughters perished in a fire; only their five-year-old son, Warren, survived. (NARA 87841.)

Maj. Gen. Arthur McArthur, who changed his name to "MacArthur" after the Civil War, was commissioned a brigadier general in 1896. He fought in the Spanish-American War and was appointed military governor of the Philippines from 1900 to 1901 during the American occupation. He died of a massive heart attack on September 5, 1912, while addressing a reunion of veterans from the 24th Wisconsin Infantry. Here, he is seen commanding a review of troops at the Presidio of San Francisco in 1904. (NARA 83641.)

Maj. Gen. Arthur McArthur was father to Douglas MacArthur, the first father and son to both be awarded the Medal of Honor. Here, Maj. Gen. Arthur McArthur is seen commanding a review of troops at the Presidio in 1904. (NARA 83640.)

Pictured here is Fort Yuma, known for its relentless heat. Gen. George C. Thomas, commander from 1851 to 1855, recollected: "One of the most disagreeable posts garrisoned by the Army . . . 116 degrees in the shade. Sleep before midnight was impossible and then only on the rooftops." (NARA 87799.)

Officers stationed at Benicia Barracks, California, in January 1896, pose for a photograph. Many of these men were later to be stationed in Yosemite National Park. Third from right appears to be Merritte Weber Ireland, who became the US surgeon general from October 4, 1918, to May 31, 1931. (NARA 103752.)

Camp Merritt in San Francisco is pictured in 1898. The camp was also known as the "Concourse," a trotting racetrack south of the Presidio and north of Golden Gate Park. It became Camp Merritt on May 29, 1898, and operated only long enough for a fleet to be assembled for the 18,000 troops disembarking for the Philippines. (NARA 82962.)

When Fort Bidwell was established in 1865, the cavalry was tasked with protecting white immigrant settlers from the Modoc Nation. The Fort Bidwell general store, built in 1874, remains one of the longest continuously operating stores in the state of California. In 1893, Fort Bidwell was converted into a government boarding school for Native American children, who were captured and forced to assimilate to Western culture. (NARA 83466.)

Pres. Millard Fillmore declared Alcatraz in San Francisco a military reservation in 1850, and by 1859, troops were permanently garrisoned at the post. About 40 years later, members of the Hopi Nation were imprisoned on Alcatraz for resisting the policy of forced education and assimilation of their children. By 1907, Alcatraz was designated a US military prison. Officers at Alcatraz are seen here in 1905. In 1969, the American Indian Movement occupied Alcatraz, marking the beginning of modern-day Native American political activism. (NARA 103753.)

Col. Abraham Kerns Arnold (pictured) was part of the 1st Cavalry Regiment, formed in June 1832 as a battalion of mounted rangers, to fight the Black Hawk War. It was officially recognized by Congress as the US Regiment of Dragoons on March 2, 1833. It held its last mounted review as a regiment of a horse cavalry on December 14, 1932. On January 16, 1933, the 1st Cavalry became the first mechanized unit in the US Army. (NARA 107680.)

Pictured are troops of the 1st Cavalry standing at inspection at Fort Grant, Arizona, in 1893. The 1st Cavalry Regiment received five battle honors during the war with Mexico. The unit took part in the Battle of Santa Cruz de Rosales in Mexico after having marched 210 miles in four days and nights to reach it. (NARA 83491.)

At Fort Washakie, Wyoming, in 1899, Troop E of the 1st Cavalry is seen training the cavalry horses to lie down. Shooting from behind the horse was rarely used in battle since it was dangerous to the rider. It is possible that scouts used this technique in order to hide their horses during reconnaissance. During the Battle of Little Bighorn, Captain Keogh's troops shot their horses in desperation to use them for cover. (NARA 83506.)

Pictured is Troop C, 1st Cavalry, at the Presidio in San Francisco on December 25, 1912. This photograph was used as the menu card for the Christmas dinner. Just a few years later, these troops were dispatched to pursue Pancho Villa in Mexico under the command of Gen. John Pershing. (NARA 106818.)

Here, Troop I of the 2nd Cavalry is returning from drill at Fort Bliss, Texas, in 1912. At this time, skirmishes on the Mexican border were constant. The 2nd Cavalry, which was eventually sent to camp southeast to protect another area, was often attacked by Villa's soldiers. (NARA 108543.)

1st Lt. George W. Goode commanded Troop H of the 1st Cavalry, was the commanding officer of Fort Yellowstone, and was designated the acting superintendent of the park, reporting to both the Army and the Department of the Interior. (NARA 105635.)

Lt. J.S. Herron of the 1st Cavalry is pictured on the left. He commanded Troop H in the field on maneuvers with the 10th Infantry, located 100 miles north of Fort Sill, Oklahoma. On his right is Capt. J.D. Glennan of the Medical Corps, who was on duty with troops as medical officer. The troops were ordered from Fort Sill to Fort Reno due to increased pressure from Indian groups. 1896 (NARA 104499.)

This is the football team of Troop C of the 1st Cavalry at Fort Riley, Kansas, in 1895. After the Pershing expedition in Mexico, Fort Riley began its Mounted Service School, which became highly regarded. Fort Riley was established originally to protect people traveling to Oregon, Colorado, Utah, New Mexico, Arizona, and California from any indigenous nations who resisted new immigrants on their land. (NARA 107687.)

Bugles and drums were used to send information quickly through the camps. A bugle call was used to assemble buglers, while reveille meant that soldiers should exit their tents and stand in formation. The stable call was meant for men to clean and feed their horses. There was a breakfast call and a boots and saddles tune, calling troops to saddle up. There were also tunes to go to bed, to go into fight, to trot one's horse, to move left or move right, to charge, or disperse. (NARA 107681.)

The 1st Cavalry camped at Helena, Montana, in the summer of 1884. From left to right are (first row) Capt. Henry Wagner, Capt. Camillo C.C. Carr, Maj. George B. Sanford, 1st Lt. Frank A. Edwards, 1st Lt. John Pitcher, and 2nd Lt. Daniel L Tate; (second row) 1st Lt. Otto L. Hein, Capt. James Jackson, Capt. Moses Harris, Capt. Albert G. Forse, 2nd Lt. James B. Aleshire, 2nd Lt. Albert L. Mills, Dr. Kneedler, 1st Lt. George B. Buackus, 2nd Lt. S. Foltz, and the contract surgeon. (NARA 104123.)

Here, Troop L of the 1st Cavalry in Fort Custer, Montana, is performing saber exercises in 1892. This troop was known as the Indian Troop. The 1st Cavalry was posted in the Western United States over a 60-year period and was tasked with annihilations and removal of people from their homes. The troop came in brutal contact with the Apache, Modoc, Nez Perce, Black Hawk, Comanche, Pawnee, Mojave, Crow, and the Sioux Nations during what is commonly referred to as the Indian Wars. (NARA 104128.)

Troop E, 1st Cavalry, at Fort Washakie, Wyoming, is training horses in 1899. The art of maneuvering a horse is the combination of placement and tension of the reins and the placement and pressure of the trooper's knees, upper legs, and lower legs. (NARA 83516.)

Troop E, 1st Cavalry, is seen here engaged in mounted wrestling drills at Fort Washakie, Wyoming, in 1899. It was extremely important to be practiced in hand-to-hand combat while working one's horse. Often, troopers fought on the ground, but keeping one's horse was preferable for safety and a competitive edge. (NARA 83517.)

Seen here is 2nd Lt. Joseph F. Herron of Troop H, 1st Cavalry, in 1896. In 1899, he was detailed for duty with the Cook Inlet Exploring Expedition, commanded by Capt. Edwin F. Glenn; the expedition was directed to find a route from the Cook Inlet to the Yukon. (NARA 105616.)

The Crow and Sahnish (also called Arikara), who were warring with the Lakota and Cheyenne, joined as troopers to assist in the extermination of their local enemy. Pictured here is a Crow trooper in Troop L of the 1st Cavalry, Fort Custer, Montana, in 1892. The 7th Cavalry was accompanied by a number of Crow, Sahnish, and Blackfoot scouts and interpreters. (NARA 104098.)

2nd Lt. Joseph F. Herron of the 1st Cavalry is pictured with his horse Kangaroo and hounds at Fort Sill, Oklahoma, in 1895. During World War I, Companies F, E, and C of the 1st Cavalry guarded the Mexican border, watching for Pancho Villa. (NARA 104493.)

Here, Troop L of the 1st Cavalry waters their horses at the Little Bighorn River, near Fort Custer, Montana, in 1892. The area is where one of the largest battles in the systematic attempt to remove Native Americans took place, the Battle of the Little Bighorn, on June 25, 1876, between federal troops and two plains nations. Lt. Col. George A. Custer led the 7th Cavalry, and Crazy Horse led the Lakota and Sioux Nations. Fighting to stop the US government's encroachment on their land and their way of life, Crazy Horse and his people won the Battle of Little Bighorn in June 1876. Custer and all his troops, scouts, and interpreters in Companies C, E, F, I, and L were slain. (NARA 104097.)

At the officers' compound at the Presidio in San Francisco, the buildings are identified from left to right as belonging to the assistant adjunct general, chief paymaster, chief quartermaster, engineer officer, post surgeon, post commander, and captain of the light battery. (NARA 87846.)

This streetscape is from Yreka, Siskiyou County, in Northern California on the border of Oregon, north of Mount Shasta. Gold miners created this town during the gold rush. Numerous tents, shacks, and a few cabins were erected quickly. The town had various names before Yreka. The 2nd Cavalry, Company M, were recruited volunteers from Siskiyou in 1861. They were first camped on the Overland Trail to assist new immigrants from attack by the area's original owners. (NARA 83702.)

The personnel of pack train No. 5 pose in Yosemite, California. US Cavalry provided protection for Yosemite National Park between 1891 and 1913. The National Park Service today still emulates the operational structure and the attire of the cavalry. (NARA 87779.)

The Fort Yuma Bridge in California crossed the Colorado River, and this picture was taken from the Arizona side, in Yuma, in 1881. Fort Yuma was established to protect immigrants to California from Yuma Indians who lived in the surrounding area. Fort Yuma, California, was located on the Colorado River opposite the mouth of the Gila River until 1851, when the fort was moved to an elevated site opposite present-day Yuma, Arizona, and on the original location of the Mission Puerto de Purísima Concepción. (NARA 82433.)

Seen here is Fort McDowell on Angel Island, San Francisco, in 1923. Fort McDowell, previously called Fort Reynolds, had been used as a recruit camp, an artillery post, and prison camp; by 1922, it had become an overseas discharge and replacement depot for processing personnel leaving and returning from overseas posts. Fort McDowell processed about 22,000 people each year between 1926 and 1938. (NARA 82440.)

The parade grounds of Fort Bidwell, California, are seen here after new construction in 1875. Along the south side of the parade grounds were the kitchen and dining rooms and some of the older barracks, which were used for storage and offices. On the north side of the parade grounds were the officers' quarters. On the west side were barracks, the commissary, a hospital, post office, and a saloon. On the east side of the parade grounds were the stables, not visible in this picture. (NARA 83391.)

Gen. Tasker H. Bliss of the US Army Signal Corps is pictured here. Bliss was commissioned a second lieutenant in the 1st Artillery and had garrison duties in Georgia and New York. He served as an assistant professor of French at West Point from 1876 until 1882. In 1885, after duty in California and Virginia, he returned to academia as an instructor at the Naval War College. (NARA 17226.)

Pres. Andrew Jackson was the strongest proponent for the Indian Removal Act—also known as the Trail of Tears—and signed the act into law. Under Jackson, over 100 million acres of Indian land were reduced to less than 32 million acres. Extermination, through military attacks, and cultural assimilation, through forced boarding schools, were attempted during this period. In California, the native population prior to Spain's invasion was nearly one million. By the end of the 19th century, it was less than 20,000. (NARA 83490.)

Gros Ventre leaders were held captive at Fort Curtis, Montana. The 2nd Cavalry Band, Companies C, D, and K, and the 11th Calvary Companies B, C, F, and H, were headquartered here in 1877. The Gros Ventres have lived around the western Great Lakes region for over 3,000 years. A farming community producing corn and other agricultural products, they lived in large cities with other Algonquian-speaking nations in present-day Minnesota and in Manitoba, Canada. (NARA 81720.)

"Cavalry vs. Indians," seen here, helped create the romanticization and justification of the genocide of the indigenous population. Frederick Remington is known for his depictions of conquering the West; this may be one of his first sketches to be published as part of Lieutenant Bigelow's journal in 1866. The image was reprinted in *On the Bloody Trail of Geronimo*, published by Western Lore Press in 1958, which continued the stereotypes of the Native Americans and the wars against them. (NARA 96838.)

The discovery of gold in California in 1848 increased the policies of removing Native Americans. Federal cavalry troops organized more attacks, and gold miners also physically removed and slaughtered Native Americans. Since the gold miners knew they would not be punished for their actions, their attacks became more ruthless. Native Americans were unable to receive justice as the state of California denied them the right to testify in court. The state also encouraged white Americans and Californios to keep Indians as indentured servants. (NARA 57-HS-909.)

The Hayden Geological Survey, funded under the Department of the Interior, was one of many mapping and geological surveys that eventually became the US Geological Survey. Ferdinand V. Hayden, MD, started exploring the northern Great Plains region around 1853. The teams were sent out to photograph, take samples, and map the American West from 1869 through 1878. These areas later became national parks, which were protected by the US Cavalry. The National Park Service still emulates the organizational structure and attire of the US Cavalry. Here, William Jackson photographs the team in the kitchen. (NARA 57-HS-950.)

This Frederick Remington sketch, "He was dragged some distance off the road," skews the balance of power between the US Cavalry and Native Americans. Images like these were used to increase funding for westward expansion from Congress and to justify the continued genocide of America's indigenous peoples. Although scenes like this did occur, events in which the US Cavalry slaughtered entire populations were much more common. (NARA RG-111-SC.)

Pictured is the 2nd Squadron, Troop F, 7th Cavalry, in Camp Columbia, Havana, Cuba, in 1898. Congress declared war against Spain in April 1898 to liberate Cuba. Members of the 1st US Volunteer Cavalry, known as the Rough Riders and commanded by Theodore Roosevelt, were some of the first to arrive in Cuba. (NARA 100845.)

Troop K of the 9th Cavalry prepares for inspection in 1898. Many soldiers in the 9th Cavalry were awarded the Medal of Honor. Sgt. Emanuel Stance was the first African American regular to be awarded the Medal of Honor in June 1870. Sergeant Stance, 22 years old, was among the first troopers to enlist in the 9th Cavalry. (NARA 85600.)

Pictured is the officers' mess for the Rough Riders while in San Antonio, Texas, in 1898. Colonel Wood and Lieutenant Colonel Roosevelt are at the head of the table. Cadet Haskell, badly wounded in the San Juan Hill battle, is at the left. Lieutenant Pershing led the 10th Cavalry in Cuba in the assault on San Juan Hill. The troopers of the 10th took heavy casualties and served with distinction alongside Lt. Col. Theodore Roosevelt's Rough Riders. The 9th and 10th Cavalry were the first established African American infantry regiments. (NARA 93574.)

Two

The Horse and the Mule

The cavalry horse was a highly trained animal and soldier. Though the rider was trained to fight without his horse, he was a better soldier with it. Cavalry horses need a considerable amount of care; farriers, blacksmiths, and veterinarians were constantly at work. The troop often had to construct their own camp, including the stables for the horses. The horses had to be fed, groomed, and watered. Food and water needed to be carried not only for troops but also for the horses. Who best to take on a burden like this but mules. Mules were invaluable assets to the cavalry regiment. Mules not only carried the water, the hay, the food, the camp building materials, and equipment on the long and arduous trek to camp, but on arrival, mules were also tasked with plowing the rain canals and gutters; pulling wagons, plows, and materials to building location sites; and performing numerous other labors.

Gen. William H. Carter, in *The US Cavalry Horse*, published first in 1895, states, "Good points in a horse are not mere matters of beauty, but shapes which, on mechanical principles, are likely to answer the required ends." He goes on to say, "Remounts for cavalry must have certain qualifications, the most important of which are the possession of sufficient mobility to execute tactical maneuvers at varying degrees of speed and the ability to stand hard service while carrying great weight."

For the cavalry soldier, being mounted on horseback is what distinguished him from other branches of military service. Having the horse, however, doubled the amount of training. As noted by Lucian K. Truscott Jr. in *The Twilight of the US Cavalry*, "it was the horse that increased the sense of responsibility of cavalrymen, for they could not forget him even for one day."

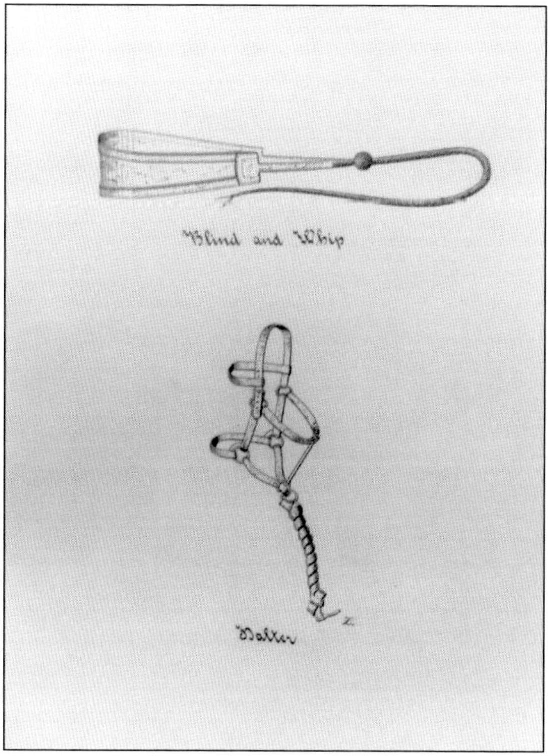

These sketches show a horse's blind whip and a halter. The halter and lead line were left on the horse for nearly all mounted activities. The halter had two sets of reins called the double bridle, the curb reins on the outside and the snaffle reins on the inside. The reins are held with the back of the hand up, a snaffle and curb around the pinky finger and the other snaffle and curb around the middle finger. The double bridle was the standard US Cavalry bridle since it allows the rider greater control and the ability to execute more complex movements of the horse. (NARA 92-P2-1-1-3 Plate 2.)

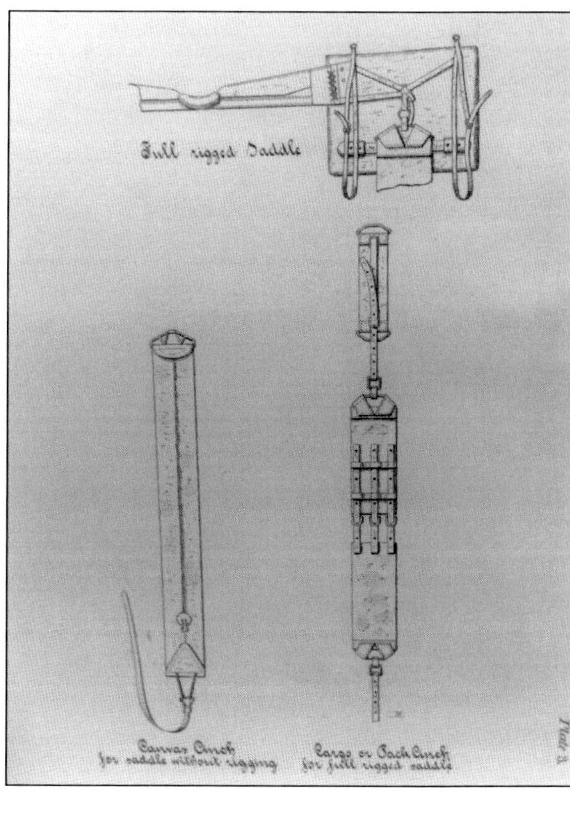

A canvas cinch for a saddle without rigging is on the left, and on the right is a cargo or pack cinch for a fully rigged saddle. The weight of an average kit is about 90 pounds. Troopers were required to carry everything they needed, except rations, on their horses to last a period of 30 to 60 days. The cavalry saddle was perfected for use in cold, tropical, or dry climates. It was made of hard woods, wrought iron, and rawhide. The saddle came in three sizes, which were 11 inches, 11.5 inches, and 12 inches in length. (NARA 92-P2-1-1-3 Plate 3.)

Here is an *aparejo*-saddled mule with ammunition boxes, showing extended drawers, one with a false bottom. The aparejo came from Mexico and was a packsaddle designed to carry extremely heavy and bulky loads. The original Mexican aparejo was made of leather and stuffed with hay or grass; it was designed to protect the mule from the load rubbing on his back and also to stabilize the weight of the pack. As part of the aparejo, each mule had a sweat blanket, and on top of the sweat blanket was a top blanket, decorated and often made of wool. This photograph was taken on April 26, 1899. (NARA 92-PS-1-3-3.)

This mule is outfitted with a stretcher on a platform saddle; H.A. Daly designed it in 1899. The stretcher was strapped to the platform, and the wounded solider was strapped to the stretcher, all of which was then attached to the mule's aparejo saddle. This picture was taken on April 26, 1899. (NARA 92-PS-1-3-7.)

Here is a fully saddled horse. The saddle appears to be the 1885 government-approved McClellan saddle. The long boot on the side is for carrying the rifle; it is positioned hanging under the rider's leg. This method throws weight on the pommel and is not comfortable for the rider and can impede the movement of the leg; however, carrying it this way is the most convenient for quick access. The saber is attached to the saddle by small straps, passing through the rings on the front end and the other through the cinch ring. (NARA 92-PS-16.)

Pictured in 1889 are examples of sling rope types, including a standing rope (No. 1), running rope (No. 2), front rope (No. 3), rear rope (No. 4), and top rope (No. 5), which all complete the hitch. When packing a mule, blankets must be clean, the saddle must be made to fit and sit correctly balanced, a cinch must be used to stop the pack from flopping around, softer items must be packed toward the animal with more angular items outside, and soft items should be wrapped around noisy items to reduce noises that might spook the mule. (NARA 92-PS-1-8.)

The aparejo has a tool pouch for the engineer corps. The metal frame on the left is used for carrying crowbars or tools too long for the pouches on either side; H.W. Daly designed this saddle in 1902. The pack train included a stevedore, a blacksmith, a cook, and 10 packers. Typically, a bell mare (a mare that all the mules are attached to and will follow anywhere), 14 riding mules, and 50 pack mules made up a train. The pack mules carried up to 200 pounds or more, sometimes placed on top of the aparejo and other times lashed to the sides. (NARA 92-PS-1-9-85.)

In *Pack Transportation* H.W. Daly, chief packer of the US Army, states, "The aparejo consists of two rectangular pieces of heavy leather sixty inches long and twenty four wide sewed together along the edges and across the middle. Two pouches are thus formed into which hay or other similar material is stuffed so as to form pads fitting the contour of the animal's body on either side of the animal's backbone." Listed here are the many accessories that made the aparejo complete. (NARA 92-PS-1-8.)

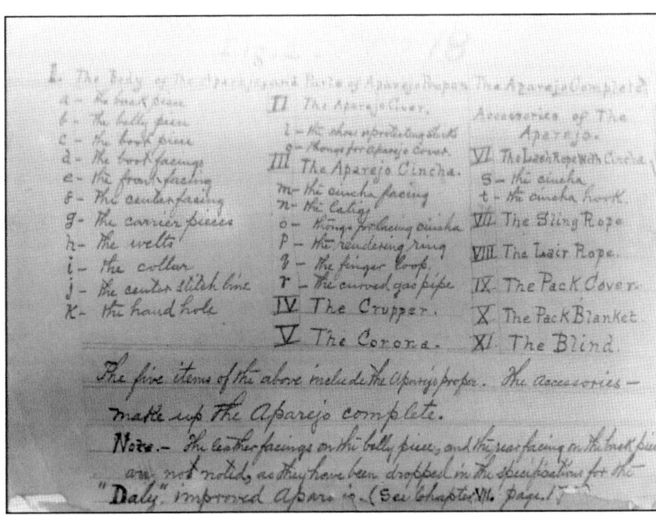

b – the belly piece
c – the book piece
d – the book facings
e – the front facing
f – the center facing
g – the carrier pieces
h – the welts
i – the collar
j – the center stitch line
k – the hand hole

II The Aparejo Cover.
o – thongs for Aparejo Cover
III The Aparejo Cincha.
m – the cincha facing
n – the Latigo
o – thongs for lacing cincha
p – the rendering ring
q – the finger loop
r – the curved gas pipe
IV The Crupper.
V The Corona.

Accessories of The Aparejo.
VI The Lash Rope With Cincha
s – the cincha
t – the cincha hook
VII The Sling Rope
VIII The Lair Rope.
IX The Pack Cover.
X The Pack Blanket
XI The Blind.

The five items of the above include the Aparejo proper. The accessories – make up the Aparejo complete.

Note. – The leather facings on the belly piece, and the rear facing on the book piece are not noted, as they have been dropped in the specifications for the "Daly" improved Aparejo [illegible]. (See Chapter VII. page 17.)

The double diamond rope tie is used for top packs. The diamond shape is on the opposite side as the hitch. The end of the lash rope is secured to the center of the side pack or the center of the top pack. It took two men to secure a top pack. Packers were civilians with experience on the western plains. They could quickly pack a mule with only a few words exchanged. (NARA 92-PS-1-9-66.)

Pictured here is the crosstree packsaddle with sling rope in position ready to receive the load. Two half hitches are formed on the front forks of the saddle, and each loose end of the sling ropes is laid over and tucked under the loop of rope. (NARA 92-PS-1-9-70.)

This mule is showing how the wooden ammunition boxes were attached to the aparejo. The Annual Report of the War Department for 1904 stated that one of the three pack saddles was arranged to carry the gun on one side, and three boxes of ammunition holding 750 rounds each on the other. The other two saddles carried a steel ammunition chest, with each chest containing seven ammunition boxes holding a total of 1,750 rounds. (NARA 92-PS-1-9-82.)

These mules are packed with straw, tents, and water. Mules were one of the most important aspects of the cavalry but rarely got as much credit as they deserved. H.W. Daly, in *Pack Transportation*, stated: "There must be intelligent or skilled packers accustomed to travel by pack, ever watchful during travel, always prompt to render assistance to the weak, to conserve their strength and be ready to meet of danger, guarding against accidents, men whose knowledge tells them the carrying capacity of every mule in their care." (NARA 92-PS-1-11-3.)

Three

A Day in the Life of a Trooper

The cavalry spent a lot of time traveling. Numerous miles were tracked across the continent and even more miles were tracked traversing north and south in the western half of what was to become the United States. Once a cavalry troop reached its destination, constructing campsites and stables and training and caring for horses were the order of the day.

However, soldiers did have time for fun, which sometimes included taking care of the camp's dogs or puppies. Lucian K. Truscott Jr. described the life of the cavalry with nostalgia and regret for those who will never experience it: "There are all too few left who respond to Stable Call or Boots and Saddles; too few who knew the warmth and glow of a cavalry stable at feed time, who knew the thrill of mounted drill or the exaltation of a thundering cavalry charge; too few who ever witnessed the magnificent spectacle of cavalry review; too few who delighted in the association with other cavalrymen."

Perhaps, with time, the more difficult days are forgotten, and the happy days are the ones that remain. The cavalry trooper was often required to march for days, often in very hot and dry weather. Some of the camps were so new that drainage ditches had to be built in case of a flash flood and bricks had to be formed and dried before the camp buildings could be built. Training was ongoing, including morning drills, inspections, and physical tests. Troops looked forward to boxing matches and mounted fighting as a way to keep fit.

Occasionally regiments would convene for field day competitions. These would include tug-of-war, the 100-yard dash, horse jumping, and blanket throwing events, as well as an interesting shoe fetching game. Often, the events included troopers from a white cavalry and troopers from a black cavalry competing together, camaraderie overcoming the prejudices and Jim Crow laws of the rest of the country.

The 11th Cavalry officers, pictured in 1916, are, from left to right, (first row) Maj. J.R. Lindsay, Lt. Col. Robert. L. Howze, Col. Henry L. Allen, Major Nicholson, Lt. Col. John M. Jenkins, Maj. Melvin W. Rowell, and Maj. Robert M. Thornburgh; (second row) Lt. Wilfred M. Blunt, Capt. William M. Renziehausen, Capt. Julian E. Gaujot, Capt. Carl H. Muller, Capt. James K. McKinley, Lt. W.F. Jernigan, Capt. Emil R. Laurson, Capt. Leon B. Kromer, Capt. Eben Swift Jr., Capt. M.C., unidentified, Lt. Burton Y. Read, and Lt. Wade Westmoreland; (third row) Lt. George B. Lake, Lt. Edwin L. Cox, Lt. William D. Geary, Lt. C.S. Hoyt, and Lt. Sumner M. Williams. (NARA 94-UMA-21-1.)

Jakie Maier is seen in front with his 2nd Cavalry Band at Fort Bliss, Texas, in 1912. The band had just returned from the Philippines, stopping first in San Francisco and then Fort Bliss. Brass bands were slightly adapted for cavalry. (NARA 108540.)

Col. Henry L. Allen of the 11th Cavalry poses in 1916. From El Paso, Texas, the 11th Cavalry was ordered to Columbus, New Mexico, to join Brig. Gen. John J. "Black Jack" Pershing and Col. James Locket in their expedition to Mexico in search of Pancho Villa. The military objective was to capture Villa, dead or alive. (NARA 94-UMA-21-7.)

Robert Lee Howze was a major in the 11th Cavalry during Gen. John J. Pershing's expedition into Mexico; it was one of the last mounted cavalry operations in Mexico in 1916. When serving with the 6th Cavalry in January 1891, R.L. Howze crossed the frozen White River in South Dakota and attacked a town of Brulé Sioux. He was presented with the Medal of Honor for this action. (NARA 94-UMA-21-8.)

Col. W.J. Nicholson belonged to the 11th Cavalry. Colonel Nicholson was first adjutant of the 7th Cavalry at Wounded Knee on December 29, 1890, where the cavalry massacred over 300 people, mostly women and children, from the Lakota Nation. He later became a brigadier general and commanded the 79th Infantry division in World War I. (NARA 94-UMA-21-5.)

Lt. J.L. Collins was commander of the 11th Cavalry. Collins was the aide-de-camp for General Pershing on the expedition into San Antonio, Texas, in 1916. An aide-de-camp is an assistant to a high-ranking officer. (NARA 94-UMA-21-11.)

Lt. George S. Patton of the 8th Cavalry is seen here in San Antonio, Texas, in 1916. It was here that Patton became known for wearing an ivory-handled Colt single-action Army revolver. Patton was known as reckless and rude but also as a formidable general, as proved by his long career in the military. (NARA 94-UMA-19-1.)

Pictured in 1916, Capt. L.L. Lawson of the 4th Artillery is standing on top of his hut. He used his roof for an artillery watchtower. (NARA 94-UMA-15-3.)

Some of the officers of Battery C, 6th Field Artillery, lived in the field. The second person from the left is Captain Pulis, who was in command. (NARA 94-UMA-16-4, 200136.)

While the troops were stationed in Mexico, boxing contests were held to keep the men active. This match took place in El Valle, Mexico, on July 5, 1916. (NARA 94-UMA-35-36, 206985.)

Field days were used as a means of continuation of training and to give the troops some competitive excitement during the down times in camp. While camped in Mexico, Lieutenant Blunt of the 11th Cavalry is pictured on July 5, 1916, jumping his horse. (NARA 203993.)

This July 5, 1916, field day event is called the resource race. Mounted men start on a signal and ride to a designated location where men are laying on the ground. The goal is to pick up one of the men and get back to the starting line with him; the first rider back is the winner. Here, a contestant heads back with his "fallen" comrade. (NARA 203993.)

Pictured is a tug-of-war event in Mexico on July 5, 1916. The *Infantry Journal* of 1915 states that one day should be set aside as a field day, on which track events, tug-of-war, and mounted potato races should be drilled. (NARA 203991.)

General Dodd (center) watches the field day events in Mexico on July 5, 1916. By 1916, George A. Dodd already had a long career, and at age 64, he was sent to Mexico to find Pancho Villa. (NARA 203989.)

The shoe race event begins with the participants across the field; at the start, they run to a box, remove their shoes, and put them into the box while a referee mixes them up. Then they must dig out their own shoes, put them back on, and run to the starting line; the first one back with both of his own shoes on wins. Here, participants are throwing their competitors' shoes off into the field, causing them to have to look on the field in addition to in the box for their shoes. (NARA 203987.)

Companies G and H are doing the blanket toss for field day activities in Mexico in 1916. A number of men hold the edge of a blanket, enough to be able to toss a single person up in the air and catch them, so that they do not hit the ground. (NARA 203769.)

This field day event involves riding a "bucking horse;" one man rides on the back of another, and the man representing the horse tries to buck off the rider. Here, the rider is being thrown to the ground in Mexico on July 5, 1916. (NARA 203773.)

Multi-regiment field day in Mexico on July 5, 1916, finished with the 100-yard dash. There were many heats so that all troops could compete. Note that field day events were not segregated. (NARA 203983.)

Building and maintaining a camp required hard work as well as skills in engineering. Seen in 1916, a plough and the trusty pack mules are used to dig a trench around the camp to help drain rainwater away from the tents. (NARA 203919.)

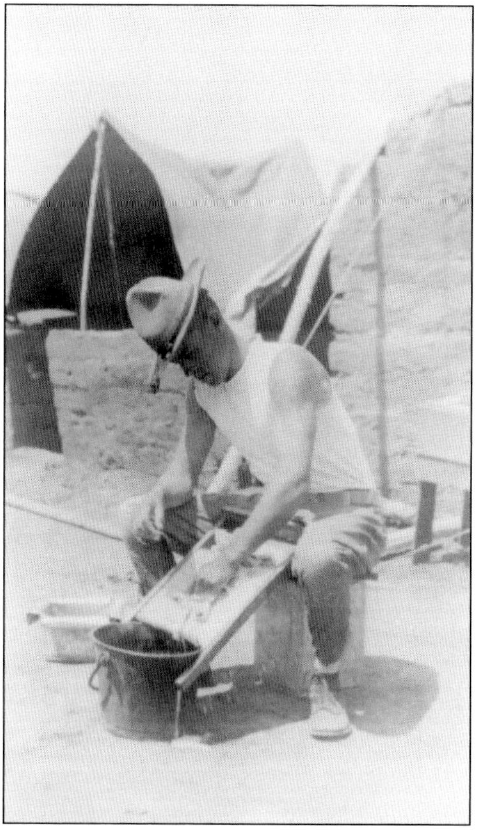

Here, a cavalry soldier is outside his adobe and canvas tent washing his clothes in Mexico in 1916. Clothes were soaked in the bucket with water and soap and then rubbed along a wooden or metal washboard. This process was repeated numerous times until the item was clean. (NARA 203949.)

This man is constructing flytraps in Mexico in 1916. Camps frequently dealt with fly infestations in the mess halls, latrines, and stables. These ingenious flytraps were used in all areas of the camp. Open wooden framed boxes were screened on all sides; flies would enter through a slit in the base and get caught inside. (NARA 208959.)

This was considered a deluxe shower. Often, sponge baths were the order of the day. Occasionally, a camp would build a shower such as this one pictured in Mexico in 1916. A man positioned on the rooftop pumped water from a barrel on the ground into a barrel on the roof, and the water could then be released by the bather underneath. (NARA 203851.)

Often camps were in communication with nearby towns, and even had working relationships with people in them. The troops stationed in Mexico during the American war with Mexico had extended periods of down time, which allowed for business relationships to develop between local farmers, restaurateurs, and other local businesses. Here are two locals come to visit the camp in Mexico in 1916. (NARA 203860.)

Often, local entrepreneurs from town would work in the camps, assisting cavalry members' spouses, cooking, or obtaining fresh eggs and produce. This photograph was taken in Mexico in 1916. (NARA 203858.)

The Machine Gun Company of the 17th Cavalry stands in front of the US flag. This picture was taken on May 25, 1916, just after the battle with the notorious Col. Candelario Cervantes, a colonel in Pancho Villa's army. Charles Brooks, third from the left, is wearing the clothes and holding the gun removed from Cervantes's body. Pershing called Cervantes "the most able and the most desperate of Villa's band." (NARA 200199.)

Here is El Valle, Mexico, camp of the 4th Field Artillery in 1916. In March 1916, Pancho Villa raided Columbus, New Mexico, instigating the assemblage of a largely cavalry. Although there were a few campaigns, for the most part, the eight months spent in El Valle were dull and boring. (NARA RG-94-UMN 206993.)

Seen here is Battery B of the 4th Field Artillery, the mountain batteries, in 1916. The men are marching into the interior of Mexico. This expedition was intended as retribution against Pancho Villa and his Villistas for their attack on Columbus, New Mexico. (NARA RG-94-UMN 207021.)

Pictured are pack mules in El Valle, Mexico, in 1916. Battery B of the 4th Field Artillery was on the way to find Pancho Villa and his supporters. Villa was a revolutionary who wanted government to redistribute land to the poor. (NARA RG-94-UMN 207023.)

Here, pack mules carrying artillery boxes take a break. Battery B of the 4th Field Artillery is on its way to find and take, dead or alive, Pancho Villa. (NARA RG-94-UMN 207024.)

Seen in El Valle is Battery B of the 4th Field Artillery in 1916. The march to find Villa's men and supporters was a hot and dusty route. Villa's men became known as Villistas during the Mexican revolution. (NARA RG-94-UMN 200173.)

Located in Mexico, these barracks made of adobe bricks were built by troops from Battery C of the 4th Field Artillery in 1916. Arriving at El Valle, the soldiers immediately set out to build mud brick huts for quarters and began to return to what amounted to a garrison routine, except for the occasional scout patrols into the nearby mountains and valleys. (NARA RG-94-UMN 204010.)

These barracks are made of adobe bricks and were constructed by troops from Battery C of the 4th Field Artillery in August 1916. Adobe brick making was an established practice in Mexico, and the cavalry borrowed the technique to make their camps. Canvas was used to create doors and awnings. (NARA RG-94-UMN 204009.)

These adobe barracks were made by Battery C of the 4th Field Artillery in 1916. Adobe bricks are made by combining mud and straw together and pressing it into rectangular molds, which are then dried in the sun. Tree logs are used to create *ramadas*. (NARA RG-94-UMN 203952.)

Here, Battery C of the 4th Field Artillery holds a drill on May 24, 1916; the pack mules appear to be carrying weaponry and ammunition boxes. The packers ensure that the load is stable and balanced. (NARA RG-94-UMN 200174.)

Major Pulis inspects field artillery pieces of Battery C, 6th Field Artillery, at El Valle, Mexico, on August 19, 1916. Field artillery had to be well maintained, clean, and in good working order. The lives of the men depended on it. (NARA RG-94-UMN 204196.)

It is payday for Battery C of the 6th Field Artillery in El Valle, Mexico, on August 19, 1916. A trooper's pay would begin at $13 per month and increase to $15. (NARA RG-94-UMN 200159.)

Pictured is payday for Battery C of the 6th Field Artillery in El Valle, Mexico, on August 19, 1916. The process of waiting in line for payday is long gone, but receiving one's wages is still looked forward to by the troopers. (NARA RG-94-UMN 200158.)

Signal flags were used when the telegraph system failed to respond, as demonstrated here by Battery C of the 6th Field Artillery in El Valle, Mexico, on August 19, 1916. (NARA RG-94-UMN 200144.)

En route with Battery C of the 5th, 6th, and 13th Field Artillery Regiments moving north from San Antonio, this picture shows the 6th Field Artillery passing through San Diego, Del Monte, in 1916. (NARA RG-94-UMN 20033.)

Battery C of the 6th Field Artillery in 1916 is marching with a camp dog trotting in front. Many soldiers had dogs in the camp, and often they would get in the way of artillery or drill practice. Lucian K. Truscott Jr. recounts an incident in which a dog, during a display of air bombers, ran into the field and chased the bombs. The dog received an engraved collar of recognition from the pilots. (NARA RG-94-UMN 20052.)

On March 30, 1916, the 5th Cavalry arrived at San Antonio, Texas, after a long march. The 5th Cavalry participated in the expedition to search for Pancho Villa for less than a year before being moved to Fort Bliss to patrol the border. (NARA RG-94-UMN 20066.)

The 5th Cavalry sets up a temporary camp in Mexico in 1916. After leaving the expedition in February 1917, the 5th Cavalry guarded the border from Fort Bliss toward Tampa, Florida. (NARA RG-94-UMN 20156.)

The Machine Gun Troop of the 10th Cavalry, the Buffalo Soldiers, is pictured here in a practice charge in 1916. It shows a full charge of horses, mules, and soldiers. (NARA 4-UMN 204059.)

Seen here is the Machine Gun Troop of the 10th Cavalry, the Buffalo Soldiers, practicing shooting in 1916. This was the start of a new era of combat. There are no horses pictured, and the men are practicing with new mechanized war equipment. (NARA RG-94-UMN 204064.)

Members of the Machine Gun Troop of the 10th Cavalry haul a sharpshooting machine gun into a tree during a drill in 1916. (NARA RG-94-UMN 204065.)

In 1916, the 11th Cavalry camped in Colonia Publan, Mexico, the present-day state of Chihuahua. In the late 1800s, the area was occupied by a Mormon colony. In 1916, the site was chosen for the expedition because of its strategic location close to the railroad. (NARA RG-94-UMN 203850.)

The 11th Cavalry is seen here in Mexico in 1916. Posing in the kitchen, a washboard is seen on the left, and pots are on the woodstove. The kitchen had an adobe brick floor and ramada-style roof. (NARA RG-94-UMN 204101.)

These troops from the 11th Cavalry are building a fly-proof dining room in 1916. To do this, screening is used for the walls and the rooftop. It was a constant battle with flies, especially near food sources and stables. (NARA RG-94-UMN 204104.)

Here, the camp is being inspected for cleanliness and order. A clean camp was a healthy one. It was essential to keep food and water clean, to remove spoiled items, and to ensure that heavy rains did not flood the camp. This is the 11th Cavalry in Mexico in 1916. (NARA RG-94-UMN 204105.)

This man is hammering the last nail in his tent, which is constructed of wood planks, canvas, and fly screen. His saddle is nearby and ready to be placed on his horse at any moment. He was a member of the 11th Cavalry, stationed in Mexico in 1916. (NARA RG-94-UMN 204108.)

This fly-proof tent was built by Sgt. M.R. Cox of Troop A the 11th Cavalry. The tent had a wood frame, adobe brick base, and a canvas top. The bricks were made on site, while the canvas, screen, and wood were carried in on the mules. (NARA RG-94-UMN 204107.)

Pictured is the 6th Infantry camp in El Valle, Mexico, in 1916. Note the adobe brick pillars with canvas-draped roofs. Some camps were constructed better than others. A lot would depend on how long each regiment thought it would be staying there. (NARA RG-94-UMN 207032.)

Here, members of the 16th Infantry are studying the parts of the newly issued Gatling gun. Captain Bohn on the right is supervising the instruction in 1916. The Gatling gun solved problems of single loading. Invented by Richard J. Gatling during the Civil War, Gatling guns, at the time, were referred to as machine guns. The Gatling gun was the predecessor for today's machine guns in that the gun loaded prepared cartridges with a hand-operated crank to allow for sequential firing. Using this new machine gun was problematic as it often had a tendency to jam and was heavy. (NARA RG-94-UMN 207053.)

The 24th Infantry is pictured in 1916 making adobe bricks to be used to construct barracks, the kitchen, mess hall, and latrines. Adobe bricks, which were common in Mexico, were new to many of the troops. (NARA RG-94-UMN 203799.)

Here, a member of Company L of the 24th Infantry has discovered that a troop dog has dug a hole and had her puppies there. Many of the soldiers had dogs with them for companionship. After entering Mexico in 1916, the 24th Infantry crossed the border again, in 1919, to engage the rebels as a measure to ensure no violence erupted across the US border. (NARA RG-94-UMN 203812.)

The 24th Infantry is constructing barracks out of adobe bricks, which took at least two days to make. Local clay was mixed with straw, shaped, and dried in the sun. Once dried, the bricks could be used in construction. (NARA RG-94-UMN 203793.)

Companies G and H of the 24th Infantry practice shooting from the trenches in 1916. Trench warfare began with the increased use of small arms. The use of trenches began in the Civil War and continued through World War I. (NARA RG-94-UMN 203755.)

A soldier of the 24th Infantry takes a break to read the paper outside his tent on July 15, 1916. In 1898, the 24th Infantry deployed to Cuba for the battle of San Juan Hill. The 6th, 13th, and 24th Infantries assaulted and seized the Spanish-held blockhouse and trench system at San Juan Hill. (NARA RG-94-UMN 203885.)

The Field Artillery of the 18th Brigade, under the command of General Hall, is practicing a surprise attack against the 79th Brigade, under the command of General Tuthill, in San Diego. This was the beginning of the mechanized cavalry; soon, the tank would replace the horse. This and the scenes that follow through page 86 took place at Camp Kearny, San Diego, on April 19, 1918. (NARA RG-111-SC, 9188.)

The 40th Division of Machine Gunners is pictured waiting for the enemy to appear in the practice battle between the 18th and 79th Brigades. At that time, wagons were used to carry heavy cannon firepower. (NARA RG-111-SC, 9163.)

Here, men take a break for chow. Bread and meat made up the order of the day, almost every day. Unlike the food on the border, the meals in Mexico could consist of tamales, chickens, or eggs. (NARA 9166.)

This soldier is eating something delicious. He is from the 40th Division, which was formed from a number of National Guard units from Western states and was designated at Camp Kearny. (NARA 9167.)

This soldier is collecting water for the troops. The camp cost $4.5 million to construct in 1917 and was in operation until 1920. The Marine Corps Air Station Miramar is located at the site of Camp Kearny today. (NARA 9168.)

143rd and 144th Field Artillery Regiments were originally the 1st and 2nd California Field Artillery Regiments. As mechanized firepower became more prevalent, the horse became less an extension of the soldier in battle. (NARA 9188.)

Here, men practice maneuvering the cannon. After Camp Kearny closed, the 40th was reconstituted in June 1926 with headquarters in Berkeley, and later changed to Los Angeles in 1937. (NARA 9174.)

Practice drills are being performed by the 143rd and the 144th Field Artillery Regiments of the 80th Brigade on the firing line in the California hills in field maneuvers. (NARA 9185.)

Practice drills are being performed by the 143rd and the 144th Field Artillery Regiments of the 80th Brigade in maneuvers against the 79th Brigade in a practice attack at Camp Kearny, San Diego, on April 19, 1918. (NARA 9188.)

At the end of World War I, the 40th, known as the "Sunshine" Division, had 2,587 members killed in action and 11,596 wounded. On April 20, 1919, the division was demobilized at Camp Kearny, where it had begun. (NARA 9182.)

Pictured are practice drills for the 40th Division of Machine Gunner on the firing line. The 40th was known as the Sunshine Division and was one of the divisions best prepared for mobilization during World War I, since a majority of the units had just been released from active duty on the Mexican border. (NARA 9183.)

Here, the 143rd and the 144th Field Artillery of the 80th Brigade are going over the tops of the California hills in practice field maneuvers. (NARA 9186.)

Brig. Gen. Leroy S. Lyons was commander of the 65th Artillery Brigade at Camp Kearny. He was promoted to major general by President Wilson. (NARA 9189.)

Practice drills included a single file crossing under the railroad tracks, which was a slow process. The railway line ran north from Rose Canyon to Sorrento Valley. Below, part of the regiment is seen having just crossed under the tracks; the rest of the regiment, seen on the right, still needs to go under. (Above, NARA 9191; below, NARA 9198.)

These troops are setting up the field's wireless wagon. Wireless meant Morse code, which was transmitted via radio waves. (Above, NARA 9192; right, NARA 9199.)

Learning the art of self-defense, these soldiers go through boxing exercises as part of their training. George Vincent Blake, a well-known and respected referee and boxing trainer, was in charge of classes. Blake was a World Boxing Hall of Fame inductee. (NARA 9193.)

The 40th Division models various types of gas masks. It was important that soldiers familiarized themselves on how to use all of them. From left to right are the American, British, French, and German gas masks. (NARA 9194.)

Mischa Elman, a famous Russian violinist born in Kiev, Ukraine, moved to America and became a citizen in 1923. He entertained numerous people from high society to the troops at Camp Kearny, as pictured here. (NARA 9195.)

Four

The Last of the 11th and the End of an Era

In 1940, two new camps were constructed in San Diego and Imperial Counties—Camp Seeley, near El Centro, and Camp Morena, near Campo. Camp Seeley was used for desert training, and Camp Morena was used for mountain and cold weather training.

By 1941, the two camps were combined into a larger single camp named Camp Lockett. Camp Lockett was named for James Lockett, who was awarded two Silver Stars for "gallantry in action against insurgent forces" in the Philippines and had been stationed there with the 11th Cavalry in 1918. After the bombing of Pearl Harbor, the 11th Cavalry and later the 10th Cavalry were stationed on the site. There was widespread fear that Japan would cross the Mexican border into California. The 11th Cavalry was led by Lt. Col. Frederick Herr.

San Diego was designated as a strategic location due to its location on the Pacific coast and the Mexican border. The decision to send horse-mounted cavalry instead of tanks was due to the rugged and mountainous terrain. Many of the hills, gorges, and valleys would have been too difficult for mechanized equipment to maneuver.

The 10th and 24th Cavalry Regiments were the last horse cavalries to be posted at Camp Lockett. San Diego's Camp Lockett was the last designated mounted cavalry camp constructed and the last active horse cavalry. The entire camp was closed on April 30, 1946, and later was used as a veterans' convalescent hospital and an Italian prisoner of war camp for over 300 people.

The shift in warfare operations from the horse to the tank was finalized by the end of World War II.

In this picture, horses and cars are used simultaneously; this was the last time horses would have such a significant role. After the bombing of Pearl Harbor on December 7, 1941, the 11th Cavalry

Regiment moved quickly to Camp Lockett, arriving only two days later.

Camp Lockett, established in June 1941, was new for these officers of the 11th Cavalry, who arrived two day after the bombing of Pearl Harbor.

Lt. Col. Frederick Herr replaced Colonel Rayner as commander. Lucian K. Truscott Jr. in *The Twilight of the US Cavalry*, describes Herr as "tall, lean and rugged . . . the picture of a Cavalryman. Active and energetic, he was a fine horseman and one of the Army's best polo players. A magnetic and pleasing personality, he was greatly admired and respected on all sides."

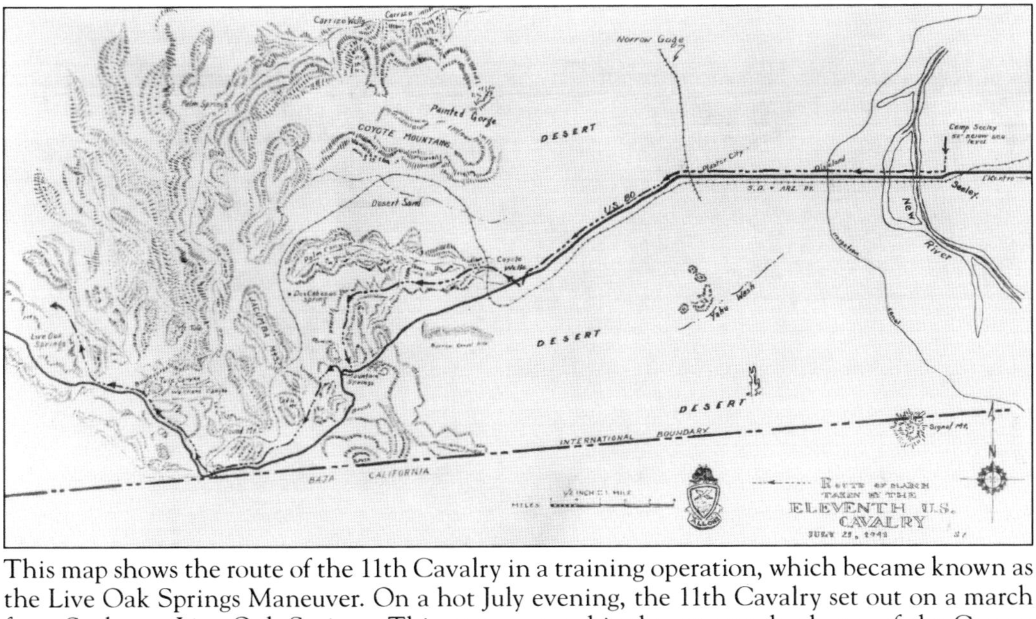

This map shows the route of the 11th Cavalry in a training operation, which became known as the Live Oak Springs Maneuver. On a hot July evening, the 11th Cavalry set out on a march from Seeley to Live Oak Springs. This area was and is the present-day home of the Campo Kumeyaay Nation.

Capt. H.J. Rosenberg recounts one particular hazardous crossing through the mountains on the way to Live Oak Springs where "the men leading pack horses with short halter shanks had to lean backwards in their saddles."

Colonel Rayner led the Live Oak Springs Maneuver, a desert march through the mountains of thick chaparral. Many of the cavalry recall the hazardous and challenging conditions of the march before reaching Jacumba, where they were able to rest before their final practice assault on Live Oak Springs.

The personnel and items on the march to Live Oak Springs, according to Capt. H.J, Rosenberg, included "Six scout cars bristling with machine guns, 684 mounted men armed with pistols and rifles, thirty officers, three cyclists armed with submachine guns, pack horses bearing machine

guns, mortars and special weapons, seventeen trucks, a semitrailer truck, a sedan, a pickup, two sidecars, and two reconnaissance cars."

After the bombing of Pearl Harbor, San Diego was seen as a vulnerable location. Ports and borders were reinforced and guarded. The US Cavalry in California was sent to protect the Mexican border. The cavalry was different from past cavalries in that there were equal parts machines and horses.

An important job was keeping the horses fed and watered. An enormous amount of grain and hay was needed to feed the horses and mules daily. At times, the amount could easily be 800,000 pounds a day, roughly 400 wagonloads. If needed, pasturage was used as a supplement for short periods.

These troops are making a few sandwiches. Making numerous sandwiches at a time was not an easy task.

Valerie Read, daughter of Myron A. Thom, recalls that Lt. Col. Frederick Herr was easy to spot, with his erect posture and his beautiful black horse.

Food lines were almost as long as payday lines. A cavalry custom for many years was waiting in line for chow. Some recall that the food was not necessarily very good, but it was always very welcomed.

Soldiers were trained to lay flat on the ground when firing; this allowed for visibility of targets while not being a target oneself. Horses were also trained to lay down.

Lines were long for dinner, and every member of the regiment was happy when he finally arrived at the pot.

Here, soldiers pose with their horses in the area that was originally home to the Kumeyaay Nation. The Kumeyaay Nation owned the coastal area south of the San Luis Rey River to Punta Santo Thomas and east from the Salton Sea into Ensenada.

With the completion of the newly built Camp Lockett and the immediate influx of cavalry personnel after the attack on Pearl Harbor, the once-quiet border town became a busy and active military post.

A corral has been quickly made with the help of barbed wire. The invention of barbed wire in the late 1880s changed land, grazing, and usage rights almost overnight. Many Native nations were restricted from normal land use by barbed wire. The mounted cavalry used it as a fast, cheap way to control people and horses.

Camp Lockett was built as a horse cavalry camp. The hills, valleys, and desert chaparral provided the perfect environment to practice drill for the horses, the soldiers, and the new mechanical cars and weaponry.

Here, packhorses carry artillery and supplies. Horses were soldiers too, and their riders knew it was important to work together. Often, horses could sense the enemy before their riders did.

A saddled horse and a packhorse walk side by side. The cavalry first occupied this site in 1878 when 16 troopers camped for several months. Then, in 1918, Troop E of the 11th Cavalry was stationed while en route from San Diego to Yuma.

On field maneuvers, the woody underbrush, rocky outcroppings, and many small streams were excellent conditions for troopers to practice battle strategies, horse and military tactics, and basic instruction.

In a prophetic image, three cavalrymen pose with a saddle pack in front of them and a covered truck behind them; it is a scene of things to come.

Saluting the colors, these men are either getting ready for review or for the field day events. The color guard presents the colors before important formal events.

Pictured are horses being tethered together. Troopers and horses had to contend with extreme climate changes. Often, the days could heat up to 110 degrees, while the night temperatures could drop drastically to 50 degrees.

Lt. Col. Frederick Herr is seen here on his horse. Herr was the "last chief of the cavalry," according to Lucian K. Truscott Jr. in *The Twilight of the US Cavalry*. Herr fought to reinstate the branch in large numbers and fought so strongly for reinstatement that he was in constant conflict with the war department.

When the 11th Cavalry arrived, members were greeted with new permanent barracks, a commissary, post office, horse stables, a hospital and veterinary building, officers' quarters, mess hall, blacksmith shops, hay sheds, recreation buildings, and a chapel.

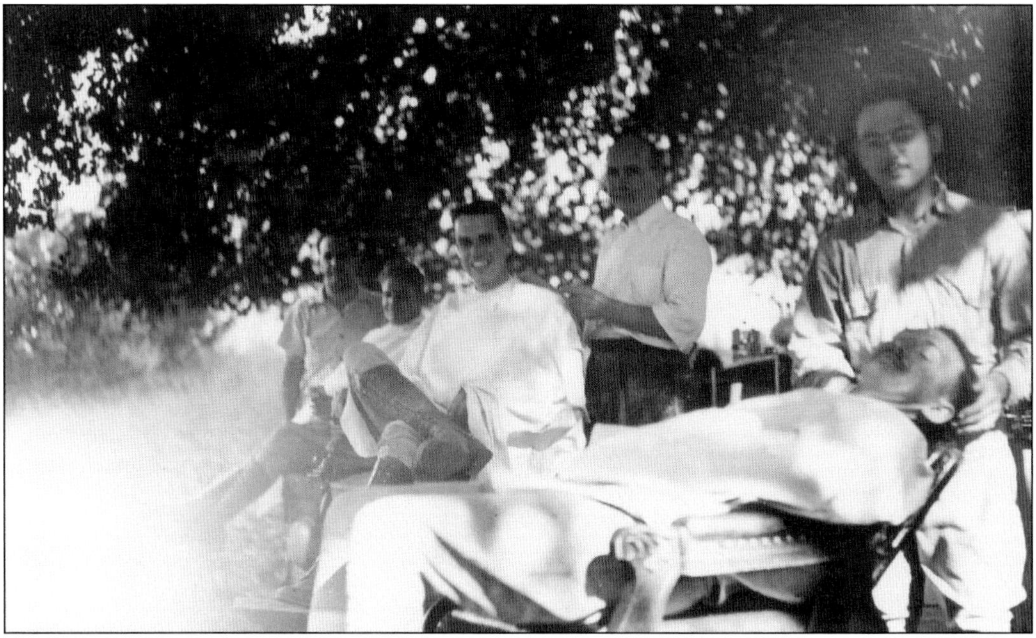

These soldiers are getting shaved in the shade. When on field maneuvers or on marches, temporary housing, kitchens, mess halls, and even barbershops had to be set up.

The mounted cavalry has a long history of camp dogs. Some pets were acquired on the way and were taken care of by one solider or often the entire troop. Dogs had been used in the military for centuries, and in World War II, they were trained to find trip wires, mines, and traps. Dogs also served as sentries.

These horses are taking a break; their saddles are in a row behind them. The saddles and packsaddles could be quite heavy. Maneuvers often meant trotting and galloping with rider and supplies.

These two soldiers are trying out the tent while on drill training.

Horses were required to respond to various commands and cues. The horses were also trained not to respond to loud noises such as gunfire.

Water for the horses was required every day when on the march, and a group was sent ahead to locate some. If the water was far from camp, the horses were sent to water in groups, which could put the regiment at a strategic disadvantage.

Practice reconnaissance missions were performed with various scenarios.

Here, men appear to be conferring and checking their maps. Sometimes going off the road required another look at the map.

Resting the horses was important too.

By 1942, the 10th Cavalry replaced the 11th Cavalry, and a year later, the 28th joined the 10th and formed the 4th Cavalry Brigade of the 2nd Cavalry Division.

Training exercises and special events became more common as the threat of imminent danger from Japan subsided. Here, the colors are presented before a review of a riding and shooting competition between troops.

During the Civil War, the cavalry horses were carefully bred Morgans and Thoroughbreds. After the westward expansion, the horses were bought from local dealers. The cavalry of the westward expansion had to find horses that could compete with the Mustang of the plains.

Water was scarce in this area, and so as part of the planning phase, the Army petitioned the San Diego City Council for permission to use water from the Morena Reservoir six miles northwest of Campo. The request was approved, and as part of the contract, the "expense of installing and operating the necessary pipeline, meter, pumps, and treatment facilities shall be borne by the government."

The man on the left is checking the time. Camps, even temporary ones, were run on precision timing. Meals, drills, and feeding and watering horses were all scheduled for thousands of men.

Mealtime means finally sitting down to eat. Meals generally included bread and various types of beans, along with bacon, beef, hardtack, eggs, and sugar.

The horse would carry the trooper's spare clothing, toiletries, rations, mess gear, horse grooming equipment, ammunition, and personal items in the saddlebags; added to that is the rolled feed bag attached to the pommel with a grain bag enclosed within.

This trooper is practicing with a machine gun on a tripod. The trooper wore the .45-caliber pistol, gas mask, and basic ammunition load; the M1 rifle was carried on the horse.

The 11th Cavalry horses are pictured around 1942 beginning their march through Campo. The town, which was close to the border, had a customs house and immigration office along with a general store, hotel, and cafe.

Myron A. Thom, in the center, holds a found cat. Myron Thom was the veterinarian of the camp, and although most of his patients were equine, a few others slipped into his office.

In *The 1862 US Cavalry Tactics*, Philip St. George Cooke emphasizes the importance of choosing a temporary campsite with the horses in mind, stating that "it is sometimes necessary to encamp without water, chiefly with view to grass."

Myron A. Thom is seen jumping his horse. Thom was the veterinarian for the 11th Cavalry. He received his doctorate of veterinary medicine from Washington State University and was deployed, along with the rest of the 11th, two days after the bombing of Pearl Harbor.

Here, Lt. Col. Frederick Herr jumps his horse. Herr was the last chief of the cavalry; he fought hard to keep the full mounted cavalry as a branch of the Army, but mechanization proved to be the downfall of the horse and the mounted cavalryman.

This was the end of an era. The last of the mounted US Cavalry served in World War II, both in America and abroad, but not in the same numbers as it had in the past. With postwar development of mechanical weapons, the US Army eliminated horses entirely from service. The last surviving tactical cavalry horse, Chief, remained on government rolls until 1968.

BIBLIOGRAPHY

Carter, Gen. William H. *The US Cavalry Horse*. Lyons Press, 2003.

Cooke, Philip St. George. *The 1862 US Cavalry Tactics, Instructions, Formations, Maneuvers*. Mechanicsburg, PA: Stackpole Books, 2004.

Deloria, Vine Jr. *Custer Died For Your Sins: An Indian Manifesto*. NY: Avon Publishers, 1969.

indiancountrytodaymedianetwork.com

McLean, James. *California Sabers: The 2nd Massachusetts Cavalry in the Civil War*. Bloomington, IN: Indiana University Press, 2000.

www.militarymuseum.org

Ottevaere, James A. *American Military Horsemanship*. Authorhouse, 2005.

Smith, Paul Chaat. *Everything You Know about Indians is Wrong*. Minneapolis, MN: University of Minnesota Press, 2009.

Truscott, Lucian K. Jr. *The Twilight of the US Cavalry, Life in the Old Army, 1917–1942*. Lawrence, KS: University Press of Kansas, 1989.

www.uscavalry.org

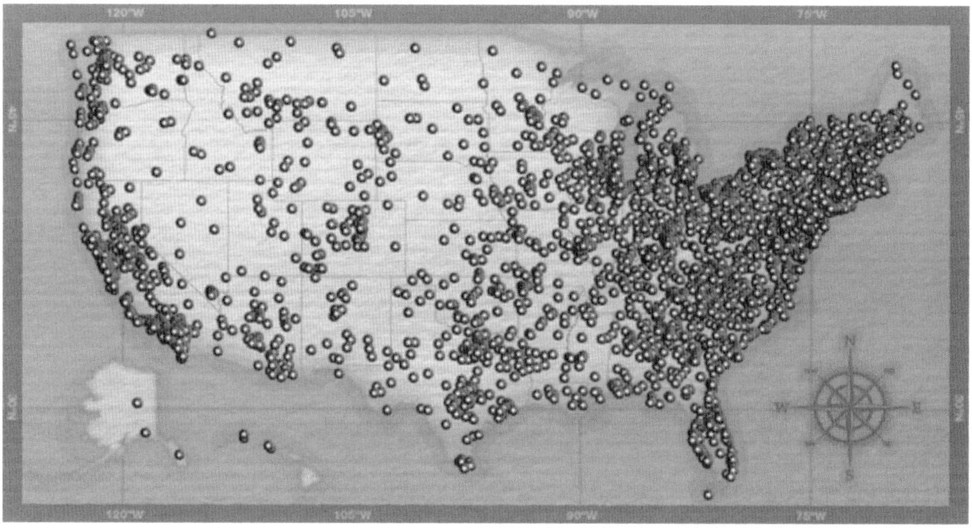